Recipes for Happiness

———————

Nigel Linacre

Published by Linacre Communications Limited
trading as Inside Out
51 St. Mary Street, Chippenham, Wilts, SN15 3JW, Wilts, England

First published by Inside Out 2007

Copyright © Nigel Linacre, 2007
All rights reserved

Design by Julia East, 2007

The moral right of the author has been asserted

This book is sold subject to the condition that it shall not, by way of trade or otherwise, be lent, re-sold, hired out or otherwise circulated without the publisher's prior consent in any form of binding or cover other than that in which it is published and without a similar condition being imposed on the subsequent purchaser.

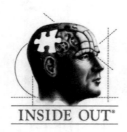

An Idea

"I want to come to England", said a Nigerian friend who had greeted me with a big smile and a peal of laughter.

"No!", I replied, "in England people don't know how to be happy", and then I had an idea...

Find out which recipes work for you.

Contents

BREAKFAST

1) Gratitude Golden Syrup
2) A Happy Cup
3) Happiness Shower
4) Mantra Muffins
5) Breath of Air
6) Posteurized Shapes
7) Tasty Toast
8) Still Water
9) Organic Refresher
10) Sunny Side Up
11) Raised Flower
12) Tender Calves
13) Friendly Pop-ups
14) Happiness on Tap
15) Soft-boiled Work
16) Birdsong Soup
17) Fillet of Failure
18) Swap Dishes
19) Dover Soul
20) Laughter Alfalfa

MAIN DISHES

21) Problem Pasta
22) The Reason Pie
23) State Banquets
24) Party Planning
25) Bubble and Squeak
26) Worry Casserole
27) Triple Chill
28) Battered Bother
29) Stir Your Own
30) Thanksgiving Feast
31) The House Speciality
32) Happy Dinner Parties
33) Happiness Hotpot
34) Mission Chips
35) Progressive Dinners
36) Donor Kebab
37) Family Supper
38) Compliments of the Chef

DESSERTS

39) Humble Pie
40) Fortune Cookies
41) OK Pavlova
42) Must Mousse
43) Jellied Feelings
44) Lottery Antidote
45) Crème Brilliant
46) Flower Flan
47) Control Crunch
48) Feeling Flambé
49) Happy Turnover
50) Regret Roulade
51) Just Desserts
52) Pat a Cake
53) Soft Sponge
54) The Plum Job
55) Sadness Crumble
56) Singing in the Rain
57) Trust Truffles
58) Home Grown Values
59) Strawberry Light
60) Mean Pie

SIDE DISHES AND SAUCES

61) Happy Sauces
62) Bon Mange Tout
63) Loving Cup
64) Happy Snacks
65) Glad Glaze
66) Unhappiness Inoculation
67) Lettuce Share
68) Critic's Choice
69) Fragrance Sensing
70) Aromatic Attention
71) Salad Bar
72) With Relish
73) Shrunken Peas
74) Like Sprouts
75) The Misery Mix
76) Fear Spices
77) Favourite Things
78) Grin and Tonic
79) Life Sauce
80) Medicinal Purposes
81) Friends
82) Happy Days

BREAKFAST

Breakfast

1) Gratitude Golden Syrup

For this recipe, you need something to be thankful for.

Thankfulness is the golden syrup of happiness. When you feel really grateful, happiness emerges spontaneously, like a bubbling stream.

Here's how to start: As soon as you wake up, give yourself a moment to notice your wakefulness and sense your surroundings. Having done that, express gratitude for the new day; it's a wonderful present.

Stir in the Gratitude Golden Syrup for everything you notice: your eyes, ears, body, your room, and so on; And it doesn't seem to matter who or what you think you are thanking. Gratitude starts your day happy.

Remember the saying: you don't know what you have got until you lose it? Gratitude helps you to know what you have got while you have it.

Happiness Hint:

Try gratitude every day for a week, if it works, continue for ever!

2) A Happy Cup

For this recipe you will need a physical object of any kind.

Select your object, for example a cup or jug. But this time notice what you may not have noticed before.

For example, notice its proportion and shape and its overall size. See any patterns and take in the overall design. Look at its colours; if there is blue, notice how that shade compares with the sky; if there is green, how does it compare with the colour of grass? Look at any shapes, are the lines soft or do they flow?

And what about the texture of the colour: is it grainy or smooth? Pick it up and notice its weight. How does it feel in your hands? How does it smell?

Notice the texture: is it soft or smooth? Uncommon sense. Take the time to notice what you notice.

Soak all of it in. It's a wonderful – if largely unnoticed – world.

Happiness Hint:
Notice the beauty that is around you and you will feel more beautiful inside.

Breakfast

3) Happiness Shower

For this recipe all you need is five minutes of quiet time.

Just as you start the day with a shower to clean your body, you can start your day with a Happiness Shower that cleans your feelings.

To prepare, get yourself into a restful place where you can sit quietly and be undisturbed. Take one or two deep breaths. Imagine that a Happiness Shower is just above your head and when you want it to it will start to shower good energy and feelings all over you.

Continue to notice your breathing as you let the Happiness Shower onto the crown of your head. As it does so, you allow it to flow all over your head, down onto your neck, collar, shoulders, chest and back, arms and legs. Let it run for a moment or two as it drains tension away, reinvigorating you.

Fortunately, the Happiness Shower comes in a portable format you can take with you anywhere you can imagine.

Happiness Hint:
*Take a Happiness Shower any time you need
a pick up.*

4) Mantra Muffins

For this you recipe will need some silence and ten minutes me time.

What you say to yourself affects your happiness. Unfortunate people listen to an internal voice that makes them unhappy with negative thoughts. But you can listen to a different voice that completely muffles the negative.

Start by selecting an "I am" Mantra Muffin that resonates well with you, like "I am happy and fulfilled", or "I am happy as I want to be". Or create your own.

Once you have got it, find somewhere you can be comfortable for ten minutes and feel OK closing your eyes so you can really focus on the sound. Start saying your Mantra internally as if you were eating and enjoying your favourite muffin. Then say it out loud as though you completely believe it.

Give it a few minutes and repeat every morning and evening for a week. If you can't initially bring yourself to say it out loud, just say it to yourself.

You may find you get an immediate shift or that you have to practise a little while longer to muffle any stale negative ideas.

Happiness Hint:
For even better results, try saying your mantra out loud.

5) Breath of Air

For this recipe you will need some fresh air, two lungs and two minutes.

The way you breathe has a huge impact on the way you feel. Change the way you breathe, and you will change the way you feel.

Before you start, notice how you feel. Next, breathe out all the air in your lungs and then take a deep breath in through your nose. Use your nose for the in-breath as the nose helps to clean and warm the air.

As you breathe in, push down on your diaphragm. That's between your chest cavity and your stomach. This will help oxygenate the lower part of your lungs too. Hold your breath for a count of two or three, or longer if you comfortably can, and then gently expel the air.

Repeat this simple cycle two or three times. Now, notice what's different. Do you feel calmer, does your mind feel clearer, and do you feel happier? Once you feel that works, you can increase the number of big breaths of air you want to enjoy.

The more deeply you breathe, the more deeply you feel.

Happiness Hint:
To add spice, blow your breath out through your mouth.

6) Posteurized Shapes

For this recipe you will need a responsive body.

Your posture constantly affects how you feel. Prepare by noticing your body. How does your neck feel? Is your spine curved or straight? Is your breathing constricted? What else do you notice? How is your gut? Sense how your posture makes you feel.

If you are able to do so, try straightening your back and neck, and gently push your shoulders down. With this posture, stand up and take a deep breath in.

Having noticed that, try gently rotating your shoulders and then your legs. Now give your arms and legs a gentle shake: what's the difference?

What you do motionally affects how you are emotionally. Become aware of the postures and body shapes that work for you. Prepare your own.

Happiness Hint:
Use motion to change your emotion.

Breakfast

7) Tasty Toast

For this recipe you need to allow a little more time to eat.

The same food gives some people pleasure and others none. Part of the difference is in how they eat.

Make more time to eat. This probably means you eat less, not more. Pay attention to the food before you start to eat it. Look at it, smell it, sense how it makes you feel. After all, you are reviewing what will shortly be part of your physical body.

As you eat, notice the food's texture and taste, and give yourself a moment to really enjoy it. The additional enjoyment is free. And food that has been really well chewed is easier to digest. What does it make you think of? When you pay attention, how do different foods actually make you feel?

Notice what you enjoy most: what foods give you the strongest taste? Which do you enjoy the most?

Even plain toast can taste really good if you pause to focus on the taste.

Happiness Hint:
You experience more of what you notice.

8) Still Water

For this recipe you need some privacy and up to fifteen minutes.

Drinking still water lubricates your body before you eat. Imbibing inner stillness helps to lubricate your emotions.

Like riding a bicycle, cultivating inner stillness takes practice. Balance may not come instantly. But taking a break from activity can yield big dividends.

Make it easier to get still by turning off the TV, radio, PC and phone, and letting any others know this is your time. Time is the greatest gift.

Start to slow down by making time to notice how you feel. Try breathing slowly. You can discover how you feel by making the time to notice how you are being.

Having slowed down, you can stop. Simply do nothing. The less you do and the stiller you become, the more you may feel and the happier you may become.

Stopping, or cultivating inner stillness, can create room for huge amounts of happiness. How do you feel right now?

Happiness Hint:
Stop human doing so you can be a human being.

9) Organic Refresher

For this recipe you will need some natural vegetation and up to an hour. For example, a park.

Start by noticing how you feel before you enter into the park. Many people have an accumulation of imbalances, energetic and emotional, that don't help.

Stroll into the park. Aim to walk at a slow and even pace. Notice your breathing and let it slow down too.

As you walk, imagine the tensions are draining down into your feet and into the park. Start with any tension that may be around the top of your head and around your eyes, and pay special attention to your jaw. Work down to the neck and shoulders where there may have been a lot of static.

While you work though your body, you may notice yourself beginning to feel a little bit lighter. You might develop a spring in your step.

The park can soak up tensions just like it soaks up CO_2. Many people have become disconnected from natural life. Try an organic refresher every day, and notice what it does for your happiness.

Happiness Hint:
The natural way to be happy is to connect with nature.

10) Sunny Side Up

For this recipe you will need regular access to sunlight.

A little sunshine goes a long way. You may have seen people popping out of buildings to get some smoke in their lungs.

Here's a better idea: pop out of any building – whenever the sun is out – to get to get a little sunshine. Inhaling sunshine is a much better idea.

Even five minutes sunshine will make you feel a whole lot better. 20 minutes a day is just about enough. And as you relax, you may actually find that you see a business issue differently.

While a walk in a park has even more benefits, five minutes on the office steps will do. And you don't have to look like you are happy: you can even look like you are thinking.

Happiness Hint:
A little sunshine on the outside helps you to feel sunnier inside.

11) Raised Flower

For this recipe you will need access to some flowers.

It's not cool to enjoy flowers. Stopping and smelling the roses isn't something that many people do. So this could seem a little unusual.

Start by finding a flower; one will do. And make some time to really notice the petals, the heart of the flower, the iris and the stem. Notice how the colours strike you. As you gaze at the flower's beauty, what do you feel? If the initial feeling is unfamiliar, or you don't immediately access a particular feeling, give it a moment or two more and let the flower start to raise you up.

Before doing this, you may wonder: what will you be doing? And in a sense the answer is: you will be doing nothing: you will be being.

Happiness Hint:
Notice how a flower opens up and you may open further.

12) Tender Calves

For this recipe you will need five minutes of time and an obedient body.

In a tense world, making time to relax is an important ingredient of happiness.

Here's a simple relaxation exercise in which you focus your attention on different parts of your body. First time around, you gently flex the key muscles in each area, second time around you simply relax there.

Start by raising your eyebrows and pulling back your ears if you can! Move the muscles around your eyes, face and jaw, and then get to work on your neck collar and shoulders.

Allow the smallest of muscle movements in your upper arms, lower arms, wrists, hands, fingers. Do the same for your chest, upper back, abdomen, gut and seat. Flex your legs, knees, down through your tender calves. Also relax your ankles and feet, right down to your toes.

Next, repeat the exercise from top to bottom with no muscle movement: simply move your attention, from the top of your head through those areas to your toes, but this time silently invite each muscle area to relax.

Happiness Hint:
To enjoy life more, drain away any stored tension.

Breakfast

13) Friendly Pop-ups

For this you will need a friend who you could call.

Start by getting in touch with a friend you haven't spoken to for a relatively long period of time. There's no need to prepare or have much to say to them, which means you won't be seeking to make a point.

In your own words, tell them that it has been a while since you have spoken and you don't have a specific reason for calling. They may jump in and say that no reason to call is a very good reason to call. Standard questions like "How are you?" often get standard answers. Unusual statements like, I was just thinking of you and I wondered how you are, may get more.

Listen closely to their tone of voice and you may sense how they really feel. Get comfortable allowing a little silence so they have room to express themselves.

Follow up specific remarks with, "And how do you feel about that?" and you may find they start to articulate at a deeper level. Listen without interpreting.

It is enough simply to pop up.

Happiness Hint:
Causing others to be happy is an easy way to be happier.

14) Happiness on Tap

For this recipe, you simply need to be present.

All you have to do to allow happiness in is to be here now. Try this: Begin by noticing where you are: you are here. And once you have done that, notice when you are: you are here now.

Notice that the past has gone, it is no longer here, and so it cannot be changed. And as it isn't here, it doesn't need to be changed. All you have are occasional selective memories.

Notice also that the future isn't here yet. All you can do is imagine a future that doesn't exist. Imagining the future you intend it may be very useful, but you are not there yet. You are here now.

Realise that what you actually have is the present, and that is all you ever have. And a great happiness recipe is to receive the present, rather than deny it. Simply allow yourself to get to know the glory in each moment.

As you accept this present, you may sense tension draining away and you will find it easier to imagine the future you are going to create.

Happiness Hint:
Happiness is always a here and now thing.

Breakfast

15) Soft-boiled Work

For this recipe you would need some work to do.

Many people think they do "hard work". What's your own view: do you think of your work as soft or hard, positive or negative, easy or difficult? Take a moment to remember a day of hard work, notice what happened, and bring to mind how it made you feel.

Now take all the ingredients of hard work and the way it makes you feel and imagine that you can put them all into a pan of water. See them all softening as you turn up the heat. If you like, decide that the boiling water turns negative feelings into positive ones.

You can throw in any other hard work stuff and see if it softens too. Some things soften quicker.

Now you may be ready to imagine a day of soft work where everything flows; make it real. Notice how you feel differently when you see yourself doing soft work. The next time someone asks you how work is, you can reply "soft".

Happiness Hint:
Whatever is bubbling, you can respond softly.

16) Birdsong Soup

For this recipe you may need to wake a little earlier than usual.

Birdsong soup is best drunk at dawn. Prepare by getting up in time to hear the dawn chorus. You will probably find it continues for an hour or so beyond dawn.

If there is no birdsong where you live, perhaps you may hear some birdsong where you work, or take a diversion into a park.

As you listen to the birdsong, try to make out the different birds' individual songs. Some sing higher, others lower. Some may have more of a trill. Notice which of their songs resonate with you.

Let their birdsongs play over and over in your mind. Rejoice in the birdsong that is all around you.

While this dish is available all year round, it is in season in spring. You may hear birdsong all over the world. We don't seem to know why birds sing; perhaps it makes them happy.

Happiness Hint:
This dish is best-served at dawn.

Breakfast

17) Fillet of Failure

For this recipe you need to think of one of your favourite failures.

Bring to mind a "failure". By all means make it one of your biggest. Now ask yourself, how is it affecting you in this moment? Right now, you may be absolutely fine.

Try another question: What have you – or could you – learn from that failure? What would you do differently next time and what difference will that make?

It turns out most so-called failures are stepping stones on the path to success. Without those stepping stones, there can be no success.

The next time you encounter an apparent failure: fillet it by noticing that you are OK. Take time to reflect on what you can learn from it and you may become stronger. Realize what you could do differently next time and you may do better. Now, thank the failure for whatever it may be teaching you. It was heavily disguised feedback.

Happiness Hint:
There is no failure, only the failure to learn from it.

18) Swap Dishes

For this recipe you need to bring to mind someone you envy or admire.

Have you ever wished you were someone else? Try doing it now and see how that works for you. By all means choose someone you admire. Imagine you have their position, their lifestyle and their character; in fact, you become them.

Because you have become them, you have ceased to exist. Everything that is special about you has ceased to be: gone, extinct, no more. How would that appeal?

Now you may realise that you are seriously attached to yourself: that there is no-one else you could be or would want to be; you are you, and that's OK. As much as other people's lives might have a superficial appeal, you are who you are, and you may even become happy about being yourself.

Happiness Hint:
All you need to be happy is to accept you are who you are.

19) Dover Soul

For this recipe all you need is a willingness to get to know yourself.

Imagine there is a part of you which you know and another part you don't know. This second part of you is deeply wise and ever-present but it may often feel just out of reach.

It tends to stay out of reach when you are determined to row your boat your way. In practice, you will only sense its presence when you want to do so.

Start by imagining that you can get in touch with wisdom, or whatever you call it, the labels don't seem to matter.

Ask it whatever you like: an important unanswered question, some guidance you want, your heart's desire. Then let go and expect an answer to pop into your mind in due course. Don't chase the answer and don't worry about it, not even for a moment. When you worry, you seem to block off the path to your soul.

Even when you open the pathway it is amazingly shy, because it speaks through virtually silent nudges, repeated circumstantial reminders, and flashes of inspiration that seem to come from nowhere at all. Awesome in power, it strives to let you be. The more often you get still, the easier it gets.

Happiness Hint:
All you need to be happy is to get to know yourself.

20) Laughter Alfalfa

For this recipe you will need something funny.

Many of us labour under the illusion that we need a specific reason to laugh. Actually we are surrounded by them and we are even funny ourselves.

But even without finding a specific reason for laughter, you can just laugh anyway. Start with a titter and gradually crank it up and you will get some of the beneficial effects of laughter. In a word, you'll be happy.

Take your own stupidities for example. What have you done that was really silly? If nothing comes to mind, you need to spend a bit more time. We've all screwed up. And as you acknowledge it and laugh about it the self-importance dissolves. You actually get to let go.

How would you describe yourself when you are laughing? Happy, surely: Get yourself ready to laugh with abandon and your cares recede.

Happiness Hint:
Laugh and the whole world laughs with you.

MAIN DISHES

Main Dishes

21) Problem Pasta

For this you recipe you need some circumstances and some strands of pasta.

Almost every problem you have ever felt you had has since disappeared, and yet you have survived. A "problem" is a mental construction around a set of circumstances. And you can change your interpretation into, say a learning opportunity and see a solution, in less time than it takes to boil pasta.

Review the circumstances in your life that seem to create a limitation and allow each of them to have a temporary "problem" label. For example, people who don't understand you, not knowing what to do about something, or simply being short of cash. Note these real circumstances and then notice that a "problem" is just a label. You could say they are opportunities: to communicate better, to figure out what to do, to make money.

To get your unconscious fully on board, imagine that each strand of pasta represents a part of a 'problem'. Put the pasta into a saucepan of boiling water. As you see the strands soften, allow that aspects of the situation are softening too. Drain the pasta and you can add your favourite solution sauce.

Happiness Hint:
Become a problem-free zone.

22) The Reason Pie

For this recipe you will need an endless supply of time.

Many people search for a reason to be happy. Actually, you don't need a reason; you can just decide to be happy anyway.

Think about it: do you have a specific reason to be happy? Try as you might, you may not find one overwhelming reason to be happy; 'reason' doesn't work like that, because it is mental. Reasons are thoughts, and happiness is a feeling.

Start to make Reason Pie by counting your blessings. Begin with anything: a body that works; a mind that can think; the food you eat; a place you have to live; friends whose company you enjoy; the list could be endless.

Put all these potential sources of happiness into your Reason Pie. Allow them to blend together and you have a powerful reason to be happy.

Happiness Hint:
Don't try to think yourself happy, feel yourself happy.

Main Dishes

23) State Banquets

For this recipe all you need is a government.

Your influence is virtually unlimited. Everything you think, say and do ripples out like waves in a pond. And your ripples influence others, and so on.

Many people are unhappy about things they don't influence. For example they are unhappy about a Government policy. While they could try to influence government policy, they don't. Instead they do nothing and complain. But how do you feel when you complain?

Start by noticing what isn't working or seems unfair. Separate cause and effect and work out what policy would need to change to get a different result. What is it that the policy-makers don't yet understand?

Become an advocate, believing that change is possible: in fact, it is certain. Policies do change, and change is brought about by change-makers.

Believe that policy-makers who haven't yet seen sense could do so. Don't think of them as enemies. They are no more stupid than you and me. It is up to you to be suitably persuasive.

Involvement in a cause in which you believe can be a cause of great happiness. You will feel more purposeful.

Happiness Hint:
Anything that isn't working is a chance to make a difference.

24) Party Planning

For this recipe you would need some goals you would like to accomplish.

Pursuing a worthwhile goal is a fabulous recipe for happiness. And imagine the party you will have when you accomplish it.

This is an extraordinary age in which you have countless choices. There is practically no limit to what may be accomplished.

Answer this: if you can accomplish anything and you know that you could not fail, what would that be? Enjoy imagining it. Visualise it as clearly as you can and ask: how will you feel when it is accomplished?

You will increase your odds of success if you are very specific about the goal. While you might have one main goal, you can have many complementary goals.

For each one of them, ask: why is accomplishing that goal important to me? In other words, what is the goal behind the goal?

If that doesn't yield enough insight, turn it upside down and ask: and what would be the impact if I don't accomplish the goal?

Happiness Hint:
Working on a goal may be as pleasurable as accomplishing it.

Main Dishes

25) Bubble and Squeak

For this recipe, you will need an out of date news medium, like an old newspaper.

Start by thumbing through the pages of an old newspaper. Notice if your eye is drawn by stories of general distress and disasters, argument and conflict, massacres and murders.

Sense how stories like this make you feel especially when they are news: anxious, tense, worried or concerned? Notice any tension in your body. The news can be a big source of unease.

Now review the impact those events have actually had upon you. The chances are that the effects were little or none. The media is simply full of the exceptions to the rule that life is proceeding fairly OK: that isn't news because it is the way things generally are. The next time you look at a news story, remember how small its impact may be.

That doesn't mean you shouldn't take up a cause that makes the world a better place; by all means do get active. But don't fret about negative news. Don't imagine that the bad things you see in the media are happening to you; because they aren't.

Happiness Hint:
Meet adversity with a happy heart.

Main Dishes

26) Worry Casserole

For this all-purpose Casserole all you need is a worry.

The recipe enables you to empty redundant worries into a slow-burning Worry Casserole where they may melt away.

Start by noticing any worry or anxiety you may have had. A recurring one would be ideal. Notice what you can about it. Does it feel dull or sharp, small or large, urgent or more distant?

Next, suppose the worry contains a message for you. Have you ever had a feeling of anxiety, and then remembered something like you left the kettle on? Well, the worry may go away when you get it. You may find that simply by asking: what is this worry about? Or asking the worry: what's your message? That you immediately get an idea, an impression, or an intuitive flash; about something you could do.

Decide if you should take action. Some worries are about things long gone. You can put any remnant of the worry into a simple casserole and consign it to an imaginary oven where the worry can melt away. Remember how delicious a good casserole can be when all the ingredients have dissolved into each other.

Happiness Hint:
The worry may go more quickly if you thank it for the message.

Main Dishes

27) Triple Chill

For this recipe you will need an over-active brain.

A happier person usually has a fairly calm mind, while a less happy person tends to have a more restless mind. As general rule, to get happier, learn how to get calmer.

There are many recipes for a calmer mind. You can chill by getting out of your mind and into the world of your senses just by noticing everything around you: a door, a window, etc., and by noticing their qualities.

Stay with each item for a moment or two and everything else will slow down.

You can chill by focusing on your breath and breathing more slowly and deeply. Really notice the breath as it moves in and out. You can chill by bringing to mind a favourite memory. You can do all three at once or one after the other.

Happiness Hint:
Let your mind do what it does and centre your attention on your body and breathing.

28) Battered Bother

For this recipe you will need a history of getting hot and bothered.

Remember times when you have been hot and bothered? Now reflect on how those incidents have affected your current situation. You may be surprised to find that in most cases, they haven't, so getting hot and bothered was a waste of energy.

So let's run the tape again in a different way. Recall a previously bothersome event but this time watch yourself – in your imagination – being perfectly calm. Follow it really closely.

You might think you can't do this. Actually, everyone can use their imagination in amazing ways. It's only a matter of practice.

You aren't rewriting the past; you are setting up the future, pouring a cooling balm over it before it bothers you.

Happiness Hint:
Notice how Battered Bother becomes more palatable when you leave it to cool.

Main Dishes

29) Stir Your Own

For this recipe you will need some happy memories.

Invest a few moments in discovering what really makes you happy, and you may be able to create that happiness again and again.

What's your happiest memory? Where were you and what were you doing? Give yourself a minute to picture it really clearly? Now here's a key question: What was it about that time that caused you so much happiness?

What did you do to create that happy time and what would have to happen for you to create similar experiences that trigger just as much happiness and more?

The more you know about what causes you to be happy, the happier you can be.

Happiness Hint:
Explore your sources of happiness.

30) Thanksgiving Feast

For this recipe you simply need to feel thankful.

It only takes a moment to be thankful and you can then feast on happiness.

Throughout the day, notice continually that you are conscious and express a feeling of thankfulness. You can be thankful for anything, you can even be thankful simply for your ability to experience the moment.

During the day notice you are where you are, and you are doing what you are doing; and express a feeling of thankfulness for that. You might find it easier to start by expressing thanks for something specific, like food and drink; a form of grace.

It doesn't matter if you have a sense of to whom or what you may be thankful; thankfulness itself seems to be enough.

You can continue expressing thanks when you remember you can do so. Many people find that feeling thankful stimulates a feeling of happiness. As anytime can work well, why not try giving thanks now?

Happiness Hint:
Thankfulness is powerful and free.

31) The House Speciality

For this recipe you will need to have memories of things that have made you happy.

Start by remembering something you have enjoyed but have not made time for recently. Allow the memories to come flooding back. You may recall visual images and sounds, and the visual images can turn into a film-like memory, as you recall actual movements. And as you remember, recall how you felt. If you felt happy at the time, re-experience that feeling of happiness.

Now ask yourself: how will I feel the next time I do this? If the answer you come up with is that you will feel happy, you have discovered one of your specialities of the house. Ask yourself: how soon and how often you can I get into this again?

Try the same recipe for each of the things you have enjoyed doing, and start to fill your life with the places, activities and people that you know make you happy. Bring them to mind and plan more.

Happiness Hint:
Enjoy your House Speciality again and again.

32) Happy Dinner Parties

For this recipe you need some people, time, and possibly cash.

Focus on making others happy and your life can become one long, joyous party.

Start by focusing on one or more people, perhaps a group, whom you would like to be happier. Reflect on the kind of event they would be likely to enjoy together. It could be as simple as a meal, or a common activity. Settle on one idea and develop it.

While you are preparing the event, invite one or more friends along to taste it. Next, issue the invitations to the feast.

Throughout the event, put your focus on enabling them to be happy. You may notice how happy you feel.

Happiness Hint:
Happiness spreads when you share yourself with others.

Main Dishes

33) Happiness Hotpot

For this you simply need your imagination and a few minutes to yourself. This recipe can work well when you are travelling on a coach or train.

Once you have read the recipe, start by closing your eyes. Imagine yourself travelling through likely future events in whatever state you would like to be in, for example, calm, happy, enjoying, and imagine the events themselves going as you would like them to, for example, smoothly.

Notice how well things could turn out and how that will make you feel. Allow that feeling to grow as much as you would like, right now. Decide that you will let events turn out just as you would like them to.

Now you can let that visualisation cook as you prepare yourself to go through those events for real. Notice how much of the day turns out the way you saw it happening.

Happiness Hint:
Prepare this at the end of the day for the following day.

Main Dishes

34) Mission Chips

For this recipe you will need a slow cooker and your most inspiring ingredients.

Before you start, let yourself gently relax.

Once you are relaxed, imagine your life has a particular purpose, even if you may not yet be aware of it. Make some time to allow the idea to emerge.

If you like, you can stir in some peace, love, understanding or even just plain happiness. Focus on people who are important to you, or draw a wide canvas. It is up to you.

Ask yourself the question: what is it you would really love to do? Initially your answer may come to you in fairly general terms. Start with the general.

Any good mission is better than none. And once you start pursuing it, you invest your life with meaning, and your whole life can feel more worthwhile.

A fabulous way to make sure you really work on your mission is to go over it in your mind every day, until it has a chip-like regularity.

Happiness Hint:
You will be very happy when you sense your purpose.

Main Dishes

35) Progressive Dinners

For this recipe all you need are some things that could get better.

You have heard of progressive dinners where you move from house to house as you finish each course. Life can be a little like that.

One of the key ingredients of happiness is whether you sense some kind of progress. So take a moment or two to sense your progress. You may think in terms of what you have done or of what you now have, of your skills or wisdom, your understanding, or even simply how you have developed as a person; whatever matters to you. If you have a sense of progress on one or more of these levels, all well and good.

But what if you don't? Then you may determine what is important to you and start working there. The main value of climbing a mountain is in climbing the mountain. The main value in developing a sense of progress is in having that sense of progress. It's a bonus when you really are getting somewhere.

Happiness Hint:
The form your progress takes is the biggest choice you make.

36) Donor Kebab

For this recipe you will need some possessions you don't really need.

In a consumer society, many people behave as though the best way to be happy is to accumulate more things. Under the weight of advertising, their houses are almost full. Strangely, they aren't always happy. Consumer happiness seldom lasts.

Look at the things that you have bought from yesteryear. Start by noticing what you have that you don't actually use. You may have grown out of it, moved beyond it, or finished reading it. Now wonder who you could usefully offer it to; a local charity shop is a great back-stop.

Notice how you feel once you have started the great give-away. If it feels good to you, get some momentum going and clear out everything that you can. The more you give away, the lighter you are likely to feel, and the happier you may get.

Give away things and you get to be happier. Give away happiness and you get to be happier still.

Happiness Hint:
When you want to have more of something, give it away.

Main Dishes

37) Family Supper

Sharing a meal with relatives can provide oodles of happiness.

Your family can be a continuing source of happiness. If you haven't got to that point where that seems possible, you may want to open up the relationships a bit. And if you don't have a family, adopt one. Treat your friends as though they are family.

Start with the intention that the whole meal will be an event. It can help to get others involved in the preparation. The food provides a wonderful context for relationship-building and repartee. Then make yourself as flexible as possible; when people really communicate something new is created, and you don't know what that will be, so you want to have a spirit of interest and wonder.

Share stories and ideas as you share the food. Listen closely to others' ideas too and look for opportunities to provide encouragement, affirmation and stimulate insight. Make sure the underlying message is one of acceptance.

Happiness Hint:
Everyone can be part of a happy family.

38) Compliments of the Chef

For this recipe you will need some people who you would be happy to get to know.

Almost every day you interact with other people, and each of these interactions can be glorious, or at least happy. This recipe may enable you to see more glory in each of these moments.

When you see your next human being, begin by noticing them. Notice their eyes, face and their general posture; hear the quality of their voice. Having done so, notice something good about them. That is a key ingredient.

Make a specific compliment. Observe closely, because if you say you look nice today, the other person may not feel that you have really noticed what is really good.

Be cautious about telling people how wonderful they are, as they are unlikely to believe you. Start with small compliments, and if you want you can work up from there.

Happiness Hint:
Make your first impulse towards other positive.

DESSERTS

Desserts

39) Humble Pie

**For this recipe you will need some self-importance,
a dicer and a blender.**

When it comes to happiness, humility is a powerful ingredient. Humility tends to nullify happiness-blocking feelings of self-importance and unimportance, like "I am better than them". A little humility goes a long way.

Start preparing Humble Pie by making yourself aware of any feelings you may have about your own importance or worth. Now imagine dicing those feelings into tiny slices. Imagine that you are just a part of what goes into the blender and you are blending yourself with the rest of creation.

Sense that you are on a par with everyone else. Essentially, you are just the same. Turn this thought over in your mind as you blend your importance with everyone else's and see if you can allow yourself to experience a strong feeling of humility. You may feel that you are no more or less important than everyone else; because there is a level at which you are just the same as everyone else. You are all part of the same pie.

Happiness Hint:
Realising you are essentially the same as others lets you rejoice in the differences. Feel humbler still.

40) Fortune Cookies

For this recipe, you will need an unrealised hope.

Whatever your circumstances, you can always dream that they will be better; and having dreamed, you can act.

Start by dreaming. If there is something that you would love to do, that you haven't yet done, what would that be?

Let it take shape in your imagination. Your dreams have to come into your mind before they go out into the world. See it happening before the eyes of your imagination, hear any sounds and notice how you feel.

Start by noticing what you most want to happen that hasn't yet happened and then notice how you feel when you bring it to mind. Does focusing on it create a good feeling, anxiety or something else?

Happiness Hint:
Your imagination is your preview of your future.

Desserts

41) OK Pavlova

For this recipe, you will need a lightness of touch.

Strangely, many people think they don't deserve to be happy. They have done things they aren't proud of, and don't realize that the same applies to the rest of the human race.

They may be miserable, but they are satisfying their need for justice. Determined to see justice done by punishing themselves, or at the very least by being unhappy. What has unhappiness done for yourself or others?

In the present moment you can forgive and be forgiven, and you can move on. Turn logic on its head and decide you have no right not to be happy. What's more, you have no right not to cause other people to be happy too.

So the moral requirement, if you decide there is one, is: cause people to be happy, starting with yourself. Imagine what your happiness can do for other people?

Happiness Hint:
Happiness is unlimited when you don't limit it

42) Must Mousse

For this recipe, you will need the "must do this" and "have to do that" thoughts.

Some limiting thoughts prevent people from being happy: "I must do this", "I have to do that", "I've got to do something". This thought-busting recipe may help you to experience more happiness and freedom.

Start by drawing together all your "must", "have to" and "got to do" thoughts. You can find them simply by writing "I must …" on a sheet of paper and then noting down what comes up, and so on.

When you have collected those ideas, toss them one at a time into an imaginary sieve that stops all the must, have-to and go-to thoughts, and lets everything good drain through. Or you can just use a bin.

For example, take the thought, "I must be more accepting", you can separate off "I must" so you just have "more accepting", and now you can substitute any more appropriate verb, e.g. "I choose to be more accepting". You can do this for all your "must" thoughts, which you can empty into an equally silly Must Mousse.

Happiness Hint:
The sieve keeps the must and lets the nourishment through.

Desserts

43) Jellied Feelings

For this recipe, you will need a range of feelings.

Your feelings can be a source of great happiness and guidance. Unfortunately, many people keep their feelings locked away where they quiver, though they may occasionally break out in tears.

Start by noticing how you feel as you go about your day. Registering small feelings is a good way to start building your awareness. When you notice that something makes you feel good, ask yourself: how do you experience feeling that good?

The phrase 'gut feel' describes a feeling that may be sensed in the gut. Where do you usually feel happiness? Once you can place it, notice how the feeling feels to you? How does it compare to jelly?

When you have an unhappy feeling you don't want to keep, just notice it and let go of it. Instead of thinking "I am unhappy", try saying to yourself: "I notice that unhappy feeling, I observe it, and when I want to, I let it go". By seeing yourself as an observer you become more detached.

Notice that feelings are just feelings. You can observe them, detach from them, go into them, and enjoy them.

Happiness Hint:
When you have an unhappy feeling, be aware of your body and the outside world and the feelings will leave.

44) Lottery Antidote

For this recipe, you would need to not postpone happiness.

Let's take a moment to review a recipe for unhappiness: lime lottery, before making a break with the lottery mentality.

For the lime lottery recipe, you would notice what you would like to have in your life that you don't have. Next, look at a lottery ticket and imagine that winning that lottery would give you everything you want. Imagine that it would give you certain feelings you want. Stop right now: lime lottery postpones happiness.

Let's move on to its antidote. Focus on a feeling that you might imagine you would have if you had won a lottery. A great feeling might be centred on your chest and spread out along your arms and legs. Your eyes radiate joy, your voice is ready to squeal with delight. How much of that feeling can you get right now? Now, imagine you can summon up that feeling any time, without ever playing the lottery.

Happiness Hint:
Start with the feeling – the rest will follow.

45) Crème Brilliant

For this recipe you simply need some wonderful memories.

Start by remembering a time when you were happy. Let your breathing slow as you take a deeper breath. As you remember that time, notice what you saw, heard and felt and let any images come to mind. And as you may begin to see any colours of that happy time, what do you start to feel?

Keeping the sights and sounds in your mind and paying attention to the sensation, double the brightness so the picture in your imagination is clearer and notice how good it feels to add some Crème Brilliant.

As you try this out, you may be learning a little bit more about how you experience happiness: through pictures, sounds or in another way.

Hang on, you may say. This is cheating. If you can just feel better without having done anything, what is the point of doing anything? You decide what you want to be different.

Happiness Hint:
Rekindle positive memories in the here and now.

46) Flower Flan

For this recipe you will need your senses and something beautiful. If you don't have access to a garden, some flowers will suffice.

In our day-to-day rush, we can overlook the beauty that always surrounds us. All we have to do to enjoy more beauty is to re-awaken our senses. This recipe may help you to experience more day-to-day happiness.

Start by noticing something that seems at least vaguely pleasant. A flower, tree or plant would be ideal. Next introduce the idea that there is beauty in what you are sensing and you are about to open yourself up to experiencing the beauty. Give yourself a moment or two in which you do absolutely nothing except sense the beauty. Providing you give yourself time to see, beauty really is in the eye of the beholder.

It is important not to want to possess the beauty. As soon as you want to have something you – by definition – do not have, you experience less happiness. Just let it be beautiful.

Happiness Hint:
Surround yourself with beautiful things in your home and notice them.

47) Control Crunch

For this recipe you would need some people who affect your life.

Some seek to control others but are unable to control themselves. This desire to control the uncontrollable creates tension and tends to squeeze out unhappiness. The recipe is to give up the need for control by becoming secure in the present.

Start by noticing the unpredictable effects other people have had on your life. Realise that they always have had uncontrollable effects and that you have managed to cope. Notice that they will continue to have an influence and you will continue to manage OK.

Imagine that the feeling of control has been in your stomach where it may have formed a knot, from time to time. As you give up your need to control, imagine the knot loosening and exiting your stomach into the space in front of you. Now imagine the feeling of control being crunched into tiny pieces.

Notice how free you feel as you give up the need to control.

Happiness Hint:
Notice how calm you can be.

48) Feeling Flambé

For this recipe you will need a negative feeling.

Many of us are burdened by negative feelings that were triggered by long-gone events. We once had a difficulty with something and we now imagine that we will have difficulties every time we encounter something similar. This recipe enables you to discover and release them one feeling at a time.

Start by bringing to mind that negative feeling. Walk back in time to the first time you remember having that feeling. View yourself from a distance. You may find you are back at a moment when it was first triggered. Viewing it safely.

As you recall those experiences, imagine that you are using a flambé to purify them, and that they are now clean and healthy. Notice that they are all gone now.

Happiness Hint:
Let go of any of the past that isn't here now.

Desserts

49) Happy Turnover

For this you will need a negative memory that may have limited your happiness, and up to ten minutes of time.

Some of our memories serve us and others don't. Memories may trigger unhappy feelings about events that are long gone. This recipe may enable you to learn any lesson and move on.

Start by remembering a time when you were really happy. When you do, notice where you were and what you were doing. Close your eyes and let the past image become clear.

Now switch your attention to the bad memory that you would like to weaken. For a last time bring it to mind, seeing the images, hearing the sounds and feeling whatever you feel. In a moment, you will close your eyes and imagine that the image flies off into the distance. As it does so, the sounds will become very quiet. When you feel ready, the tiny image will simply evaporate into nothing. Ready? Give it a go.

To sweeten, focus on the place where the previous image disappeared, and let a new dot form that encloses the positive memory you had a few moments ago. Let that positive image grow in size as it comes towards you, together with any sound and feeling. Ready? Your sweet is served.

Happiness Hint:
Sweet memories nourish and heal sour ones.

50) Regret Roulade

For this recipe, you would need a past event that you regret.

Start by remembering an event that you have regretted. Something you did or something you didn't do.

Run it through your mind one last time from the beginning right through to the end and on to any consequences, noticing any bitter taste. Got it?

Now, fold the memory into an imaginary roulade that entirely drowns out any negativity with your favourite strong flavour. Imagine so much taste.

Learning from the past can be healthy. Regretting the past is unhealthy. Though you may not be able to change the past, you can change your relationship to it, expressed by how you feel. Keep digesting the roulade.

Happiness Hint:
Regrets regress you, projects progress you.

51) Just Desserts

For this you would need to have a history of which you aren't entirely proud.

Sometimes we exceeded our expectations and sometimes not. And that is perfectly OK.

But some of us like to give ourselves a hard time for not always doing well. If we have upset someone else and we feel sorrow about that, we can do what we can to make things better or we can give ourselves a hard time. And some people do.

Typically, they console themselves with the thought that at least justice is being done. But there's a better way.

Give up trying to dispense justice to yourself or others. And just do what you can. You will feel a whole lot better. Don't try to give yourself your just desserts. Enjoy the desserts that are all around you.

Happiness Hint:
Take off that judge's wig and let your hair down.

52) Pat a Cake

For this recipe all you need is to have accomplished something.

Many people are their own worst critics: quick to criticise, they overlook their own accomplishments, and they often behave similarly towards others. This recipe may enable you to lighten up and give yourself the occasional pat on the back.

Every day, you accomplish things but how often do you stop to acknowledge what you have accomplished. The next time you accomplish anything, it could be as small as catching a train in good time, give yourself a metaphorical pat on the back. Just take a moment to enjoy that feeling.

The more you give yourself a pat on the back, the more such cakes you will bake. Once you have given yourself a pat on the back, give someone else a pat on the back too.

Happiness Hint:
Pat a Cake is a vital part of your daily reality check.

Desserts

53) Soft Sponge

For this you simply need an interest and some time you can regularly dedicate.

All you have to do to escape all unhappiness is to forget yourself. And it is easy to forget little old you when you become totally absorbed in another activity.

Abstract yourself from the present with an interest that declutters your mind. All of the mental chit-chat simply stops as you soak up something else. You can't be unhappy about anything else when you aren't thinking about anything else.

So start by finding something that interests you and you believe you could enjoy. It could be church-bells or chess, football or photography, shell-fish or stamp-collecting. It doesn't matter: what does matter is that you get absorbed in it.

Practise this something so that you gradually develop your knowledge and skill. Spend periods of time in single-minded concentration and you may find that the rest of the world, with whatever interest it may have in unhappiness, ceases to exist, just as you do, and a gentle feeling of happiness starts to emerge.

Happiness Hint:
Happiness is fostered by doing what you truly enjoy.

54) The Plum Job

For this recipe you would need to want a particular job or position.

Many people seem unhappy about their work but don't have any plans to change it.

Actually, you can flip both of those beliefs: be happy with the way things are and have a clear view of how you intend things to be. For example, suppose you don't yet have the ideal job.

First, notice everything that is good about the job you currently have. If you don't see anything good about the job: maybe that is telling you something about yourself; or maybe having the wrong job will act as a spur to you to get another job. Either way, you can learn.

Second, clarify the job that would make you really happy. What do you love to do? What are you happiest doing? What do people tell you that you are really good at?

Third, if there is no absolute obstacle, decide to get the job, and start to develop a clear plan to do so. Fourth, whether you feel ready or not, start to put the plan into action.

Happiness Hint:
If you aren't happy about something, take action.

Desserts

55) Sadness Crumble

For this recipe you would need a feeling of sadness.

If sadness may come upon you like a wave, it can move on equally quickly. Letting feelings ebb and flow is a key to happiness. This recipe may enable you to do so more easily.

Remember a recent feeling of sadness. What was it like: As you remember it, does it feel like it is in your head, or your heart or your stomach? If the feeling had a cause, what would the cause be?

Acknowledge that possible cause and then imagine that the feeling of sadness is gently crumbling and falling away until it is now in pieces on the ground.

If you sense there is still some sadness inside you, let that crumble too; now, notice how you are feeling.

Happiness Hint:
Sadness usually depends on a memory of past events that no longer exist.

56) Singing in the Rain

For this you simply need a voice and possibly a little privacy.

How do you feel when you sing? Many people don't immediately know because they haven't sung in years. They even imagine that they can't sing.

But singing, even singing in the rain, is likely to cause you to feel happy in minutes, especially if you sing with gusto.

Start by taking a really good in-breath so you really fill your lungs. Actually, a few deeper breaths even before you start will give you more singing power.

Choose a song that you know, preferably one that already has some meaning for you. An uplifting song is more likely to uplift you. And now focus on the first few words and on the count of three, breathe in and give it a good blast: one, two, three: Sing!

Singing does many things that are likely to cause you to feel happier. To start with, you tend to breathe more deeply, which would produce calm without any further effort. Second, you actually get to make a sound. Third, as your singing improves, you get to hear something rather lovely. "What a glorious feeling, I'm happy again!"

Happiness Hint:
Sing and the world resounds more beautifully

57) Trust Truffles

For this recipe all you need is the time you have.

Many people are anxious about a future that they can never know. But in the present, there is no future to get to know only a future to create.

You may have noticed you have survived every apparent crisis that has come your way. They may even have made you stronger.

In all probability the life you are living right now will continue for many more years. The question is: what difference will you make? How will you use your skills and capabilities to make a powerful difference? It doesn't really matter what happens to you, only what you happen to do. Try focusing on that and taste the difference.

As you shift your focus from your needs to what you are actually creating, you may find that you are able to develop a greater level of trust. Imagine you could eat a trust truffle that would spread trust throughout your being.

Trust is one of the most rewarding qualities to develop. It's a big happiness-builder. Trust that all is well, that all will go well; trust in the present.

Happiness Hint:
Trust things will go as you intend and respond when they don't.

Desserts

58) Home Grown Values

For this you simply need some things in which you believe.

Any conflict between the way you are living and your deeply-held beliefs may limit your happiness, but exploring what you really believe in is rarely done well, let alone put into practice. This recipe may enable you to do so.

Start by asking yourself: what do you really believe in? What is actually important to you? Until you do this, you may have been going along with other people's values without a clear sense of your own.

These will become your Home-Grown Values, and they are likely to help you to understand why you do what you do and what you would really love to do.

Gather together all the values and rank them in order of important to you, with the most important value first, and so on. Once you have your list, start from the top and check that the first one is more important than the second one, and so on, all the way down, reprioritising as you go along, until you have your Home-Grown Values.

Happiness Hint:
Home-Grown always tastes best.

Desserts

59) Strawberry Light

For this recipe you need your senses and someone to sense.

People are inherently wonderful. For a moment, imagine no-one existed at all: there would be so much to miss.

Start by noticing someone else. As you sense more of the wonder in every living thing, you tend to feel much happier. This recipe may help you to feel wonderful.

When you are with someone, drop your preconceptions. Forget your thoughts and anxieties of the moment; even forget your feelings about them and simply be present. Breathe gently and enable yourself to get still.

Look at them softly. Don't try to focus on particular features: soften your gaze until you can get a sense of the person as a whole. You may start to sense how wonderful they really are. And then allow that sense to step inside.

Try sensing the light within. Everyone you meet has a light within them. Even though you may not see it, it is the light emanates from their heart. Think of it as strawberry-shaped. Make a little effort to feel it: You have one too.

Happiness hint:
As you see wonder in others, your own wonder is revealed.

60) Mean Pie

For this you simply need some curiosity.

Some people search for the meaning of life. Rather than search for the meaning of life as a whole, you could focus on the meaning of your life. And rather than search for a meaning out there, you could create one in here.

Start by supposing your life does have a meaning that you have not yet discovered. Imagine you are in the world for a reason even though you may not yet know what it is. Suppose your life could become hugely purposeful. Where to start?

Notice what gives you the greatest pleasure: what you are actually doing when you are at your happiest of all, when everything just flows. What you most love to do may be close to your purpose.

Consider what you would most like to create if you could? What is that and what will it look like when it is done? And what have you been telling yourself that you couldn't do but you would love to do if you could?

Consider how you can bring more of that into your life and your happiness is likely to grow.

Happiness Hint:
The meaning of your life is the meaning that you give it.

SIDE DISHES
&
SAUCES

Side Dishes & Sauces

61) Happy Sauces

For this recipe you will need a seemingly bad event.

The circumstances that surround you are as they are. Within them, it is possible to be happy or unhappy, or anything else. In this recipe, you can pour a happy sauce on events and transform them.

Start by noticing the event, for example, some milk has been spilt on the floor. Notice the typical feeling this has tended to provoke. Now prepare the happy sauce by imagining that this is an opportunity even if you don't yet know what that is: for example to encourage the milk-spiller by letting them know that such an event is really trivial; or to get in there and show how you can mop up milk with a smile. Every event is an opportunity to realise something.

Realise that it's never what happens that matters; it is always your response that makes the difference.

Throughout a day, you may notice dozens of everyday events that could be interpreted as being bad or good. Grab your happy sauce and apply it lavishly to the troubled area it will transform many dishes.

Happiness Hint:
Change the flavour of any experience by adding this sauce.

62) Bon Mange Tout

For this recipe you need a moment to appreciate.

Actually sensing each moment rather than being constantly wrapped up in the past or the future is a key to happiness.

Start by noticing that you are in the present and now is all there is. After all, the past has gone and the future isn't here yet.

To make really good mange tout, trim away the past and the future so you are left with an awareness of the present. As you do so, suppose that you are also trimming away any regrets you may have; which are always about the past. At the same time, you are trimming away any worries you may have; which are always about the future. You can easily trim the past and the future away because the present is all you need. In fact, it is all you directly experience. As you experience it, it turns out that the present is an amazing gift, because it comes complete with everything you need for each moment.

Try it for yourself: right here, right now, do you have all you need for this moment; and for this one and this one. If you find yourself saying, "Yes, but what about ..." notice that it doesn't exist, and return to the present. And the present is good: as you eat Bon Mange Tout, you can taste the whole moment.

Happiness Hint:
Pause now for five seconds to allow yourself to enjoy them.

Side Dishes & Sauces

63) Loving Cup

Giving and receiving love is bound to engender happiness.

The best way to receive love is to give love, and giving love turns out to be as rewarding as receiving it. While the ultimate is to love and be loved by others, there are several preliminary steps.

Start by accepting yourself. Realise that you are the way you are. Though your character may unfold as your awareness increases, change takes time, and can seldom be forced.

Once you have got to a point where you accept yourself, try loving yourself; little old you is as lovable as anyone else. You would do yourself no favours by not loving yourself. And you are likely to become more lovable as you accept more love into your life. To become more loving, you must let more love in. Having got more comfortable with the idea of loving yourself, you may be ready to love other people more. The good news is you can give love in all kinds of ways.

Start by imagining sending them a feeling, you can do this whether they are physically present or not, be a bit more direct by giving them a loving look; a gentle acceptance given from a place of calm. Go further and share a loving cup. Let every relationship grow. The loving cup is something you will want to drink for your own sake.

Happiness Hint:
Love one another as you love yourself.

Recipes for Happiness Nigel Linacre

64) Happy Snacks

For this you simply need the odd minute that doesn't have to be filled with activity.

Punctuate your day with instants in which you stop to have a happy snack.

Start by stopping whatever you are doing. Slow everything right down until you are willing nothing to happen at all. You are simply being.

Doing nothing as you notice your lungs continue to breathe and your heart beat. And in this moment, which may be any moment, you may sense how wonderful it is simply to be.

Think of your favourite thing. Bring to mind someone you love. Call someone whom you care about. Punctuate your day with instants in which you stop to have a happy snack.

Incidentally, if you notice your mind doing its chatter thing, just bring your attention back to your breathing and take a deeper breath.

Happiness Hint:
The only time to be happy is the present.

65) Glad Glaze

For this recipe you need a busy urban street with a lot of pedestrians. A busy pedestrianised shopping street is ideal.

Happiness can be mildly infectious. A highly effective way to experience more joy in your life is simply to cause other people to have more joy in their lives. You can do this surprisingly easily. In this recipe, you can discover how to do so any time you encounter strangers.

Start to walk down the street. As people walk towards you, simply notice each one of them with a quick glance and as you look towards them silently wish them happiness. You may notice which of them seem troubled.

You can think of each wish as being a blessing. You can imagine a feeling extending out from you to them. It doesn't matter if you don't manage to wish happiness to everyone you see, just give a silent wish to as many as you can manage.

Happiness Hint:

Spread happiness on thick

66) Unhappiness Inoculation

For this you will need yesterday's newspaper.

The media amplify the unusual. While billions of people go about their untroubled lives, exceptional events are centre stage. Some onlookers fret, and start to feel troubled themselves. This recipe may enable you to separate yourself from the exceptionally negative.

Yesterday's newspaper will provide plenty of examples of disputes, murders, and environmental calamities. Notice the events themselves without reacting in any way. Then notice that it would normally have triggered a negative reaction in you, and perhaps a negative belief, like "People don't care".

Next, shift your focus. Notice if the reported news of yesterday really affected you. Almost always, the actual effect will have been zero. Realise that any negative thoughts that might have been triggered by yesterday's events would have been unnecessary. The same applies to apparently negative events you may hear about in future. Reading old newspapers helps you to get perspective. You may not experience a feeling of urgency or compulsion as you read out of date papers, but who wants to experience urgency or compulsion?

This doesn't mean you do nothing about news. Happily, you can take action, but becoming unhappy is not an action you need to take.

Happiness Hint:
Notice that most of the world is at peace with itself.

Side Dishes & Sauces

67) Lettuce Share

For this you simply need some people with whom you can communicate.

Happiness is self-replenishing. The more of it you give away, the more of it you have. In fact, the more you give away things, the happier you tend to get. People who think they are unhappy because they are scared of losing things are usually unhappy because they are hanging on to them.

Start with the intent of causing the next person you communicate with to feel happier. Continue with the next person and so on. You might give them a smile, a really sincere "How are you?" or you might simply listen closely to them.

It may not matter whether you can see that you actually achieve it in every case, because your intent is transformational. Every time you meet with someone there is an interchange of happiness or unhappiness.

You may be conscious of sensing how they are. With practice, you may experience the feeling they are feeling, so make sure they are feeling good.

Happiness Hint:
The more you give away happiness the more space you create for more happiness.

Side Dishes & Sauces

68) Critic's Choice

For this recipe you would need to pay limited attention.

Most people have an inner voice that continually criticizes them. It says things like "I am no good at ...", "I always have problems with ..." and so on. Often you can hear it popping out in the language that is used. What if you could quieten that voice and even enable it to be constructive. This recipe may enable you to do so.

Start by absent-mindedly noticing your own internal voice. Sense when it is being critical. Carefully notice its volume, pitch and tone of voice. Now it is time to have fun.

Become a careless listener. Notice what happens when you increase the pitch, so it becomes a high, squeaky voice. Notice what happens when you turn the volume down so it becomes relatively far away. Imagine the voice disappearing into the distance as the volume heads all the way down to silence. What happened to the critic?

Happiness Hint:
Create your own voice of happiness.

Side Dishes & Sauces

69) Fragrance Sensing

For this recipe you would need time to sense perfection.

Start by tuning in to your senses. Notice what you see, hear, taste and smell. Try amplifying this by paying closer attention to each of your senses in turn.

Take a moment or two to look at the world that is around you now. Listen to all of the sounds you can hear including any that you may not have been hearing. Take a deeper breath and notice any smells you can register, do the same with taste. Finally, notice how your stomach and heart feel.

As your senses bring your awareness into to the here-and-now, you may encounter a sense of relative stillness. In this stillness you may notice that everything within your experience is OK; and all is well because you have realized that you are OK. As your mind has become less turbulent, take a moment to be untroubled.

Nonsense arises when people are cut off from their senses. They get stuck in some imaginary past or future. Most of all, they get stuck in their heads: come to your senses.

Happiness Hint:
To be happy all you need to do is come to your senses.

Side Dishes & Sauces

70) Aromatic Attention

For this recipe you will need someone you can listen to and up to ten minutes of time to give-away.

There is so much to notice in other people. The more attention you give them, the more they will feel appreciated, and the happier they will be. The more happiness you can give, the more you will receive.

Start by noticing the other person. Even before they start talking to you, notice how they are. Use your eyes to look into their eyes, notice their face and sense any tension. Listen to the tone of their voice, and sense any strain that may be in their voice.

As they talk, suppose they are articulating only part of what they feel, and that there is more to come if you give it room. Pepper the conversation with the shortest of communications like "And ..." that simply invite them to add more. If they use an unusual word like "struggle", simply ask, "Struggle, what is that?" In general, give them space by being as silent as you can.

Throughout this time, you will have been giving them what they most need: attention. And because of this they will feel valued, and that will enable them to feel happy.

Happiness Hint:
Pay attention to others from your heart.

Side Dishes & Sauces

71) Salad Bar

For this recipe, you simply need to have made a number of choices.

Your life may seem to contain a haphazard set of circumstances. By looking closely, you may notice that at some level you invited them into your life. Once you realised you invited them in, you can notice what else you might like to invite.

Start by reviewing the ingredients in your life. Notice how each one of them got there. In each case, you probably thought about something, said something and did something. And hey presto, the circumstances are with you now.

Life is like a salad.

Realize that you are free to make more choices. In fact, you can't avoid making them, including the choice of keeping something as it is. As you clarify just how free you really are, you may experience a tingle of anticipation.

Happiness Hint:
Decide on your favourite salad and start to gather the ingredients.

72) With Relish

For this recipe you will need some water, some privacy and up to fifteen minutes.

Do whatever you do with Relish and you will feel more alive and more passionate.

Many of us have been rushing through life as though it is an interlude. Some of us eat and drink in the same way, treating meals as mere pit stops. Actually, you can turn the smallest thing into a happiness-producing event. It all depends.

Start to drink the water, and as you do so, determine to follow it as it goes down your throat. Notice how far you can continue to sense it until it is out of reach. Enjoy feeling good inside.

Do the same with food. Eat with relish and you sharpen your senses.

Happiness Hint:
Noticing how we nourish ourselves adds to our happiness.

73) Shrunken Peas

For this recipe you would simply need a negative memory that you want to defuse.

Start by bringing the negative memory to mind as clearly as you can, and remember that you are in charge of your imagination.

Allow an image to form. Notice if you are in the picture you are imagining or if you were, as it were, in yourself looking around. If you were in yourself, move out so you can observe yourself, and then put the image of yourself up on a movie screen.

Next simply allow the screen to shrink so it gets smaller and smaller until it disappears. As it gets smaller allow any sounds to quieten until they are silent too. Gone? Good. For persistent memories, shrink the screen several times over.

This will help you to really understand that the events you have been rehearsing are no longer around.

Happiness Hint:
Accentuate the positive, eliminate the negative.

Side Dishes & Sauces

74) Like Sprouts

For this recipe you will need to remember something or someone you don't like.

Disliking anyone or anything tends to make you feel worse. Liking anyone or anything tends to make you feel happier. Liking everything and everyone tend to sprout happiness all over the place.

Can you remember someone you don't like? Start by bringing an aspect of them to mind that you don't much care for. Now just silently say: "I forgive you for being like that" and notice any change in the way that you feel. Now focus on some aspect of them that you could like, however trivial it may be. As you do you can allow yourself to feel good about that and feel better.

When you feel good about other people, you feel good. It's as simple as that. You may say that you don't feel good about someone and that may be true at the time, but who gains from your not feeling good about someone? Not you and not them.

When you let everyone off whatever grudge you may have had, it is you who makes the biggest gain. So it's time to like sprouts.

Happiness Hint:
Change the inside and you start to change the outside.

75) The Misery Mix

All you need for this recipe is someone who is unhappy and a half-hour.

In your journey to happiness, you won't find that everyone is as happy as you. The issue arises: will they pull you down or will you pull them up, or will you both stay where you are?

Imagine that you have just met someone who is unhappy: yikes! Rather than impose your happy feelings, it may feel more appropriate to acknowledge how they are. You may respond to their unhappiness with your attention, interest and concern.

But notice that their feelings belong to them, and as you encounter them, you can let the feelings wash past you, rather than climb in the pit of misery yourself.

Listen closely as you let your friend tell you about her or his unhappiness. And stay happy.

Happiness Hint:
Other people are entitled to their feelings.

76) Fear Spices

For this you would need to be aware of fear.

There's a wonderful thing you can do that can diminish any fear. Face it and ask yourself: so what if it happens?

You will get to the fear behind the fear. And once you have got to that one, ask yourself the same question again: so what if it happens? And you will get to the fear behind that one, and so on and on.

When you do this, when you actually observe your fears, you may be surprised to find that you are getting calmer. After a while, you may get to a point where you discover the source of the fears, and you may then decide to do something about it, you may actually become sufficiently motivated to take action!

A fear that you face can bring spice to life and prompt timely action. An unfaced fear may niggle away, weakening you and becoming an obstacle to your happiness.

Happiness Hint:
Digest fears as quickly as you do spices

Side Dishes & Sauces

77) Favourite Things

For this recipe you will need any negative feeling you are ready to eliminate.

Your unconscious has huge impact on your state of mind. Fortunately it is possible to communicate with it. The unconscious mind is most easily influenced by images.

Start by noticing a negative feeling and take some deeper breaths. Notice the whereabouts of the negative feeling. Like a gut-feeling, suppose this negative feeling has a centre that you are about to locate.

If a place doesn't spring to mind, just work through different areas that you can eliminate, e.g. arms, legs, until you come to a place where you may sense resistance. Suppose the feeling has a colour and notice what colour comes to mind; trust that the first colour that comes to mind will represent it. Notice what texture the feeling would have, if it has a texture.

Once you have found it, think of the colour of your favourite food. Allow the negative feeling to change colour so it starts to become the colour of your favourite food. Keep working on it until it has completely changed colour because you are in charge of your imagination. How did that change the negative feeling?

Happiness Hint:
Negative feelings are there until you let them go.

Side Dishes & Sauces

78) Grin and Tonic

For this you simply need your imagination and a few minutes to yourself. This recipe can work very well when you are travelling on a coach or train.

Many people unwittingly limit their happiness by carrying tension. They picked it up when they did something that made them feel tense, but they didn't release it and it hasn't gone away. Favourite places for storing tension include the jaw, neck and abdomen. This recipe may help you to slough off tension.

Start by noticing any tension in your jaw and drain it away. Do the same with the muscles around your mouth. With your lips pressed gently together, gently lengthen them, curling them slightly upwards at their edges, so that you have made a toothless smile. Separate your lips and gently lick the upper side of your lower lip and the lower side of your upper lip. Your lips should naturally separate so you have formed a smile.

In itself, this will almost immediately give you a tonic. Depending on your taste you may find you gain happiness by grinning throughout the day.

Happiness Hint:
To create happiness in our lives we need to take care of our bodies.

79) Life Sauce

For this recipe you need some causes and some effects.

Are you happening to life or is life happening to you? If life seems to be happening to you and you aren't happy with the way that it is, you may have unwittingly adopted a victim mentality.

Start by noticing an area of your life you are unhappy about, notice it came about, and realise the role you played in its creation. Look carefully, and you may notice that you allowed into your life everything that is here now including your partner, friends, the work you do and where you live.

Look at any areas of your life that seem negative, own up to your role, and notice what you have learnt or could learn from each of them; especially look for learnings about yourself. You could take the view that each of them is there to teach you something.

Imagine that you can take the idea of being a victim and toss it into a simple sauce, where it melts into nothingness.

What do you expect to come into your life next? Notice your invitation, and get ready for its arrival.

Happiness Hint:
If you don't like the effects, change the causes.

80) Medicinal Purposes

For this recipe you would need some space.

Imagine that there is a space between the sometimes apparently turbulent world and you. The existence of this space means that whatever happens in the world, and plenty of stuff happens every day, it need not affect you at all. You can choose your own weather.

As you get to know this space, you can increase your sense of personal calmness: so how do you get to know it?

Start by noticing your breathing, and now slow your breathing right down and notice the space between the out-breath and the in-breath.

Your breath mediates between you and the world. It regulates your response to it.

And as you move into a slower way of breathing, with regular spaces, you move into a meditative and restorative state that has wonderful medicinal purposes.

Happiness Hint:
All you ever need to be happy is to control your breath.

81) Friends

For this recipe you will a friend who is willing to give you some time.

Friends and family can make a huge difference to your happiness. What has to happen for this to be a consistently positive experience?

Start by making some time to be with a friend. While there can be happiness amongst the noise, there can be even more happiness in companionable silence. Even during conversation, notice how the silences feel. Sense if you can get a deeper connection. Look into your friend's eyes during the silence and notice how powerful that may feel. Just look in wonder and you may start to feel wonderful.

You might encounter a feeling of acceptance. It could even feel like love. As love is all around you, you don't need words to communicate. The feeling will do.

Realise that the content is secondary. The experience of being with a friend is enough to feel fabulous.

Happiness Hint:
Make time for your friends without an agenda.

Side Dishes & Sauces

82) Happy Days

For this recipe you will need a day you can focus upon.

Prepare this recipe the night before and you are likely to have a happier following day. Letting your unconscious know what you intend is a powerful way to enable events to flow. The upshot is usually a happier future.

Start by simply previewing the coming day through a happiness lens. Imagine how the day will go if it goes well: what will happen and how. See and hear the forthcoming events and you lock on to those possibilities. Your unconscious mind will encourage you to behave in a way that is consistent with events occurring, increasing the chances that they will come about exactly as you see them.

This is very powerful because most of your behaviour is in fact unconscious. Unfortunately, experience suggests this process can also work in reverse, when people expect things to go unhappily and find that they do.

As you complete your positive preview, allow a happy feeling of anticipation to build. See if you can register a feeling of trust that events will occur in a way that works for all concerned. This will get easier as you practise more. Now, you have a happy day.

Happiness Hint:
Intend future events to flow in a happy way.

Nigel Linacre loves to hear from his readers, and particularly the insights they get having read his books and listened to his cassettes. Mail info@happinessworks.co.uk.

Nigel Linacre enjoys life. His mission is to enable people to lighten up. Literally.

He coaches with the leading coaching practice Inside Out. He has worked in more than ten countries in four continents. He speaks at events. Anywhere a show is wanted.

His previous titles are 'Advertising for Account Handlers' and 'The Successful Executive'. He is currently completing a book about the riddles of life entitled 'Why you are here. Briefly.'

And the support team

Julia East designed this book, Charlotte Linacre developed the cover idea. Thank you to Sue Linacre whose enthusiasm will bring anything to life, Vaughn Malcolm meditation teacher for many turns of phrase, Malcolm Small whose courage knows no bounds, Brendan Llewellyn for making it all more positive, Trish Henry for nurturing, Jamie Denton who coached the idea into print, all my clients for so many insights, Paul Santus whose character is inspirational, and Martin Palethorpe who wouldn't let go.